Best-Kept Secrets of Major League Pitching

Larry Monroe

ISBN: 1-58518-871-9
Library of Congress Control Number: 2003110341
Cover design: Kerry Hartjen
Text design: Jeanne Hamilton
Front cover photo: Ed Betz/Pool/Getty Images
Text photos of Major League Baseball players: Tony Inzerillo

Coaches Choice
P.O. Box 1828
Monterey, CA 93942
www.coacheschoice.com

Dedication

To my wife, Jaine, whose love and support make every day better than the day before.

To my children, Taylor, Allison, and Grant, who make me proud to be their father in so many ways.

To Alexandra and Rachael, whom I have come to love as my own.

To my sisters, Barb and Diane, and my brother, Greg, thank you for cheering me on and showing me what family means through the years.

And to my parents, Bob and Lorraine, whose love and support made me what I am today.

Acknowledgments

I would like to thank a countless number of people for their contributions to this book. Many of them don't even know how much they helped. First I would like to thank my wife, Jaine, for giving me the inspiration to sit down and write this for the youngsters everywhere who want to pitch. Thanks to my children Taylor, Allie, and Grant who have all had to endure my over-analysis throughout the years.

Thanks to Jerry Reinsdorf, the owner of the White Sox, for giving me endless opportunities to increase my knowledge and allowing me to expand on my beliefs. He has always taken great care of me and my family and is one of the greatest, most caring men I have ever met.

Thanks to my bosses over the years with the White Sox, including Ron Schueler, Roland Hemond, Dave Dombrowski, Larry Himes, and Ken Williams, who all taught me so much about baseball and life and gave me the freedom to learn and expand my horizons. Thanks to all the pitchers I have coached and talked to, along with the numerous coaches I have spent many late nights drinking colas and arguing about the right and the wrong way to pitch.

I have acquired much of my knowledge from the tremendous pitching coaches and scouts we have with the White Sox. Our constant analysis and exchanging of ideas have been a tremendous learning experience for me. These men are the best in the business and are the main reasons the White Sox have a continuous flow of quality pitchers who come through the system. Thanks guys for putting up with all my questions and challenges through the years. Pitchers are indeed blessed if they are fortunate enough to be in the White Sox system.

Most of all, I really want to thank all of the coaches out there who give up so much of their time and effort to make better players and better people. Without all of you the game would not be so successful and popular. Tom Seidel was my high school coach and got me started on this obsession for pitching and to him I am eternally grateful.

Thanks to my high school principal, Jack Martin, for being a mentor and friend and for editing this book.

My special thanks to Tony Inzerillo for the beautiful and professional pictures that he allowed me to use for this book. Major League baseball gave special permission to use these photos to better illustrate the techniques that are explained and shown in this book. The people in the Commissioner's office were especially helpful and gracious, with a special thanks to Don Hintz for his help and Marc Jenkins from the White Sox who helped secure the rights to these pictures.

Lastly, but most importantly, I want to thank my parents, Bob and Lorraine, who always encouraged me to succeed and supported my decisions. I am only sorry that they are not with us any more to see this book. I can only hope as many young people out there have parents, coaches, and mentors as I have had who will help them reach their goals.

Preface

The writing of this book was a labor of love. Every material thing I possess in life is because of baseball. I was chosen by the Chicago White Sox as the eighth pick of the first round of the 1974 draft, and I left for the rookie league in Sarasota, Florida the day after graduation from high school. I am still with the White Sox, and I feel so fortunate to have been with such a great organization for nearly 30 years. Most people in my profession have not been as blessed as I have.

My experiences, from the first trip to the mound to the present day, have been an education. I have played with, coached, scouted, and met some of the greatest players ever to play the game. From all these people and situations I have learned so much about the game and, specifically, about pitching, that I felt a need to pass it on to other generations. I wish that I had known a lot of these things when I began my career.

In 1976, at the age of 20, I was called up to the Major Leagues and pitched in 11 games. I had some success and some failure, but the experience of pitching in the big leagues is one that can hardly be matched. I tore my rotator cuff the following season, and at that time, they couldn't repair shoulders as they can today. I have always wondered if I could have prevented that injury if I had known more about the proper mechanics of pitching delivery.

That thought has compelled me to write this book. I want every young pitcher out there to understand not only how to be the best he can be but also how to pitch without suffering a major injury. The factors that I explain in my book are proven ways to be a successful pitcher *and* to do so with the least risk of injury.

Too few people in baseball today understand the correct way of pitching, and it hurts me to see many young pitchers, both professional and amateur, doing things improperly. They either will not reach their full potential or will get hurt in the process. With that in mind, I attempted to address much of this book to those players who are in their formative years.

Much of my message was gleaned from talks with baseball personnel and from my administrative duties with the White Sox. When I headed the Sox's minor leagues in the early 1990s, I had many pitchers to watch and learn from. Pitchers who made common mistakes could not progress, and some became injured.

This loss of valuable personnel caused all of us in the organization to examine those flaws and to seek solutions in our developmental programs. The White Sox have subsequently had a continuous flow of young pitchers succeed. It was from this learning process that this book was born.

I promise that if you follow the instructions detailed in this book you will become the best pitcher you can be. We in the baseball community spend countless hours discussing all these points to make the pitcher better. Over the years, some great pitching coaches such as Pat Dobson, Don Cooper, Dewey Robinson, Dave Duncan, Kirk Champion, and Curt Hasler have taught me alot. In turn, I feel that I am obligated to pass that knowledge on to you.

I have attempted to address all ages in this book, from beginners to professional pitchers. Nothing is more exciting to me than the confrontation between pitcher and hitter. Keeping control of the game by what you do on the mound is the ultimate challenge. Once you learn to do this, then hopefully I will be coming out to watch you pitch in the Major Leagues.

Table of Contents

Introduction

It was one of those cloudless summer afternoons in upstate New York, where any outdoor activity would have been enjoyable. However, on this particular August afternoon in 1974, the Chicago White Sox were playing the Atlanta Braves in the annual Hall of Fame exhibition game in Cooperstown, New York. Henry Aaron had just passed Babe Ruth on the all-time home run list. Aaron's name in the lineup had changed this normally meaningless contest into a major attraction.

I had just turned 18 the previous June and was the number one draft choice for the White Sox that same month. As I signed the contract, they asked me to be the starting pitcher in Cooperstown. Little did I know that one of the first Major League hitters I would face would be Mr. Aaron.

The stands were filled with fans who erupted at the mere mention of Aaron's name. It was clear they were there for one reason—to see the all-time home run king. They had never heard of Larry Monroe, nor did they care. It was all I could do just to walk to the mound and keep my feet straight. I had never been so nervous in my life.

As I finished my warm-up pitches, I settled on two goals. Number two was to throw strikes and not embarrass my team, my parents, or myself by walking a parade of hitters. But the number one goal was to keep Hammering Hank from hitting a home run off me.

When third baseman Ron Santo tossed me the ball to start the game, I could see him chuckling behind his mitt. As I tried to figure out why he was laughing, I heard a thunderous ovation from the crowd. It was then that I realized the joke was on me. Aaron wouldn't be *one* of the first batters I would face; he would be the *first*.

I turned to face home plate and saw that all so familiar vision of Aaron, a classic pose which has transcended generations. He was digging his hole at home plate and adjusting his helmet at the same time. I knew that I was going to face him, but did he have to lead off? It turns out he was going to participate in this exhibition for a few at bats and then leave. Was I looking at the same schedule?

My first pitch bounced on the plate, and my second was way outside and up. These fans were not there to see number 44 walk, and I tried to throw a pitch right down the middle of the plate. I figured that a home run to Aaron would be better than a riot. He hit a sharp grounder through the hole between shortstop and third base. The crowd roared, and I can say that it was truly the first time in my life that I was very happy to give up a single.

On Aaron's second at bat, he singled to left again, and since the left field wall was only some 260 feet away, I considered this more than a minor victory. Between innings our manager, the legendary Chuck Tanner, suggested that I try throwing Aaron a change-up to get him out on his front foot and maybe reach for the ball.

I had been a dominating high school pitcher, throwing just a fastball and a curveball, and had never thrown a change-up in my life. I tried to imagine how to throw one, and I certainly didn't want to admit my ignorance to anyone. So, the third and final time I faced him I got him to a 1-1 count and threw a change-up that was more or less a slow straight fastball. Sure enough, the all-time home run king reached out and hit a high towering fly ball that didn't get past Santo at third base.

In retrospect, I realize that I threw a pitch that I had never thrown before to the man who at that time was the most prolific home run hitter *of all time, and I got away with it*. Maybe that was the beginning of my lifelong interest in the *game inside the game*.

That 1-on-1 challenge between pitcher and hitter can be one of the simplest encounters between two opponents, or you can make it the most complicated. This confrontation is the *essence* of baseball. The more you can understand about the intricacies of this battle, the more you can appreciate the game itself.

It was also an awakening to what lay ahead of me if I were to be competitive at baseball's top level. Despite the fact that I had been blessed with energetic Little League coaches and a very knowledgeable high school coach, there was much I didn't know.

Once I discovered that there was a science to pitching, however, I approached the job much the way any scientist does, beginning with observation. I studied other pitchers and watched how they threw certain pitches successfully. I realized better body control increased the amount of pitches they could throw effectively and improved their overall placement of the ball.

If their balance over the rubber in their delivery was good and the direction of their movements was straight to the catcher, the command of their pitches was good. Unnecessary movements or spinning off the target when they threw led to lack of control and inconsistent break of their pitches. I set my mind to achieving the mechanics necessary to throw four pitches and get control of them.

There was much trial and error in my practices. That is, I would try different grips on the ball and watch how it reacted as it neared the plate. I would try to *feel* my delivery as I practiced my pitches. When I threw a bad pitch or did not throw it where I intended to, I would recognize why it had happened. I developed a feel for pitching, instead of just winding up and throwing as I had done before.

It took time and practice, but eventually I commanded my pitches to the catcher's glove with some consistency. In 1976 when I played AA ball in Knoxville, Tennessee, we went to a four-man rotation, meaning the starting pitchers threw every four days instead of every five days as most rotations are now. On the middle day between starts, we threw batting practice for 10 minutes. In batting practice, I did not try to throw as hard as I could but instead threw with about an 80-percent effort. I worked on having a smooth delivery with as little effort as possible and attempted to throw strikes to different sections of the plate so the hitters could hit them.

I learned from this practice that the majority of time the hitters hit many groundballs and lazy fly balls that would have been outs if it were happening in a real game. Big discovery! Placement of the ball got hitters out. Control of the strike zone meant more than just throwing the ball over the plate. Natural movement of the fastball was enough to prevent a hitter from centering the ball on the bat.

By pitching every fourth day, my control improved greatly. I went from walking about five hitters every nine innings to walking two per nine innings.

Consequently, I improved rapidly and got called up to the White Sox on August 12 that same year. I was much better prepared to face the challenges at the Major League level because of that experience.

Despite all that I learned to that point, I often was too stiff in my delivery, causing me some arm problems. It was then that I began to pitch with more fluid mechanics, but the injury to my shoulder had diminished my skills too much for me to compete in the Major Leagues.

After trying to pitch for three more years, I realized that I would not make it back to the majors and retired as a pitcher. I became a scout for the White Sox and through the years experienced many aspects of baseball. This work in the game gave me many chances to learn all about pitching from a different perspective. It taught me why some pitchers never achieved consistency to their stuff and never made the big leagues. It also helped to inspire me to pass along this knowledge in this book.

Understanding all of the intricacies of pitching takes time and observation. Your career will take many twists and turns and will involve times of success and times of failure. Watch Major League pitchers on television and see how their delivery dictates the command of their pitches. Greg Maddox is the best example of a pitcher who has a simple delivery with very little effort but with great mechanics and direction. This allows him to easily place the ball in the strike zone, whereupon the batters get themselves out. One of the primary purposes of this book is to provide you with the "ingredients" necessary to pitch to the best of your ability.

The mechanics of pitching that are addressed in this book are not absolutes. However, after pitching, coaching, and scouting in professional baseball for some 30 years, I strongly believe that proven methods exist for consistency and effectiveness. The more of this process you master, the more successful pitcher you will be. This book addresses many aspects of the art of pitching, everything from standing on the rubber, to the point of delivery.

The delivery detailed in this book is intended to help you be consistent. It is directed mainly to starting pitchers. Starters must do things consistently well, because they throw more innings than relievers and must throw different pitches for strikes. The reliever can get away with fewer quality pitches for a shorter amount of time. While all pitchers should practice proper mechanics, if you plan to be a starting pitcher, it is even more important that you acquire the mechanics reviewed in the following chapters. When perfected, adherence to these mechanics will provide you with the most effective delivery you can learn and will help make you successful over the years. *Keep in mind, the more you control your body movements and your direction to the plate, the better control you will have overall.*

1

Throwing Hard, Throwing Down

The art of pitching begins simply enough. From the time you are children, your instinct is to pick up a ball that was on the ground, wind up, and throw it. It is your parent's first indication of which hand is your dominant one.

As you get older and start to play organized baseball, you have to throw a ball over the plate to keep the game moving. Over time the game speeds up, and the players get better. It becomes an art of locating the baseball in places over the plate or near the plate where the hitter will not make solid contact.

One major hurdle for a young pitcher to overcome is the mindset that every pitch must be thrown as hard as possible or that a breaking ball has to be the sharpest breaker he has ever thrown. This power mentality often ignores the ultimate goal—to get the batter out. To be successful, a pitcher not only has to keep the power mentality but also has to maintain control and balance of his movements.

The professional scouting community is obsessed with how hard an individual throws in determining if a prospect is worthy of a contract. The assumption is that at the very least, a *minimum* velocity is necessary to cut down the reaction time of a hitter. Major League hitters are so quick with their hands that the longer they have to react to the thrown ball, the better chance they have of centering the ball on the bat and making solid contact.

The most effective way to keep hitters from centering the ball on the bat is to change the velocity of a pitch to make them swing too late or too early. If the velocity on the pitch is high, the hitter will tend to react late and not catch up. If the velocity is slower than the hitter expects, he will be early with his swing and have to slow down his bat to make contact.

The other way to avoid solid contact is to have the ball change altitude as it nears the plate so that the bat will be below or above the ball. Making the ball rise is a skill most people do not possess; however, getting the ball to sink or drop as it nears the plate is something anyone can do if the ball is thrown properly. The later and sharper this drop occurs, the less reaction time the hitter has to center the ball and make solid contact. One of the goals of this book is to help you acquire these skills on a consistent basis.

If a young pitcher has enough velocity (90 miles per hour on a speed gun), professional people believe that he can then be taught to throw the other pitches, make the ball move, locate the ball in the strike zone, and be a successful Major League pitcher.

A velocity lower than 90 mph decreases the margin of error that a pitcher has and gives the hitter more time to react and a better chance to center the ball on the big part of the bat. Because velocity is basically a natural talent over which you have little control, you must find a way to use the most of your ability to become as effective as you can. This book assumes that any type of pitcher has ways of improving his weaponry, including his velocity.

Besides velocity, throwing so as to create a downward plane to the plate is important to effective pitching. Height is a definite physical advantage in developing this skill. Most of the top Major League hurlers are 6'2" and taller, enabling them to throw the ball *down* to the plate without pushing the ball on the same plane.

Vertical angle and movement are key factors in minimizing the ability of the hitter to center the ball on the bat. The reason why the pitcher's mound is in the middle of the diamond is because the mound creates a natural downward plane to help the pitcher. The ability to use this edge to your advantage is paramount to reaching your full potential. Some individuals in the baseball profession have considered raising the height of the mound to give pitchers a greater advantage, because the number of runs scored has been increasing steadily for the past 20 years. This consideration is indeed an indicator of the importance of using height to your advantage.

The downward plane is simply the path measured from the height of releasing the ball to the height the ball is when it reaches the plate. If the ball is released by the pitcher at seven feet above the pitcher's mound and it reaches the plate knee high to the hitter, the ball has gone downward at least seven feet, given the height of the mound. This change of planes to the batter's eye makes centering the ball on the bat more difficult. The more difficult you make it for the batter to center the ball on the bat, the harder it will be for the batter to hit the ball solidly. This factor is the reason that the more successful pitchers tend to be taller and stand taller on the mound throughout their delivery.

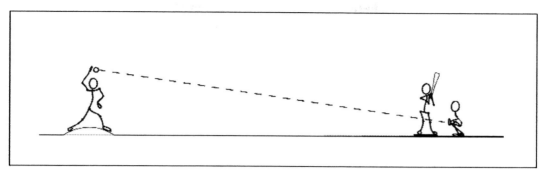

Figure 1-1. This figure shows the downward plane. The ball is released above the pitcher's head on top of the mound to the level of the hitter's knees. This angle makes it more difficult for the hitter to canter the bat on the ball. If you imagine the pitcher squatting and releasing the ball from a lower point, it decreases the downward angle, and the hitter must only time the ball to make solid contact. If the pitcher then adds late depth to the pitch, it will be even more difficult to make solid contact.

It isn't necessary to be tall in stature to pitch successfully. You can become a good pitcher no matter how tall you are. Some of the greatest pitchers of all time were less than six feet tall, such as Bobby Shantz and Whitey Ford. Using all of your height to your advantage is the important factor in creating an advantageous angle. Whatever your height, the downward plane is a major factor in your delivery of the baseball.

Simply put, the more adjustments you force the hitter to make, the better your chance for success. Hitting a baseball that is traveling downhill makes solid contact more difficult. The success of a relatively tall pitcher, such as Randy Johnson, illustrates the difficulty in hitting a ball that comes from such an angle. Of course, you'll find many other reasons for making good pitches, but this is one that cannot be overemphasized. Throwing the ball at 96 miles per hour and making the ball move late as Johnson does also helps quite a bit. But, even if you can't throw hard, the downward plane can help you be successful. *Maintain your downward plane to the plate no matter what your height is, and you will maximize your effectiveness as a pitcher.*

2

Delivery Mechanics

This chapter examines the physical act of throwing a baseball, hopefully for strikes. It is a pitcher's manual for the proper mechanical approach to delivering a baseball. Look closely at this process and practice the fundamentals.

Gripping the Ball

Your index and middle fingers should always be on top of the ball when you throw, and you should eventually get the feel that the fingertips are the last point where you touch the ball. In the normal process of throwing the ball, your hand goes over the top and around the inside of the ball. This factor is what causes the ball to have a tailing action, the natural movement to a thrown ball, and if yours moves differently, your release is different than most.

Figure 2-1. This photo illustrates a fastball grip with the fingers together. The seams are under the fingertips.

It is necessary to monitor this movement for possible change. The thumb of your throwing hand is something that can have a great effect on your pitches. Because your index and middle fingers should *always* be on top of the ball, your thumb should rest under the ball. When practicing your pitches, experiment with your thumb placement to discover how your pitches change.

It is different for every pitcher. You should practice placing your thumb loosely on the bottom of the ball. You may feel more comfortable holding your thumb firmer on the ball. Experiment with gradually sliding your thumb a little up the side or under the ball. Do not let your thumb slide too far up. Keep in mind that a minor adjustment can be more comfortable and more effective. This process is an individual's choice and usually involves some trial and error. Play with the ball in your hand while practicing, and find the grip that is best for you.

Figure 2-2. Pedro Martinez of the Boston Red Sox has his index and middle fingers on top of the ball and his thumb under the ball on this fastball.

The size of your hands has a lot to do with what will make you comfortable. Since the size of hands differ, you should try many different grips. Once you find one that is best for you, stay with it. Each pitch may have a different thumb placement or pressure, but when throwing each selected pitch, you should get consistent on how you throw that pitch. The ball will act differently with your thumb placement, but be sure your thumb doesn't cause you to get around the ball.

Figure 2-3. Mark Buehrle of the Chicago White Sox with the same grip as Pedro Martinez. This is the proper grip for a fastball.

Figure 2-4. This picture of Tom Seaver, when he was with the White Sox, clearly shows how the index and middle fingers go over the top and inside of the ball when throwing a fastball. This happens naturally and should not be a forced action.

It is fun to practice grips when throwing the ball. Most youngsters hold the fastball with their fingers split a little on top of the ball because of their lack of strength when they are young. As you reach your teens, begin to bring your fingers together and feel how the ball leaves your hand. You should watch how the ball reacts as it nears the plate. You may develop two or more different movements to your fastball as you experiment with these grips.

Most youngsters separate their fingers on the ball but as your hands and fingers grow and your body becomes stronger, you may find that putting your fingers together will give you more control and power. Each grip you try will have a different result, and you should learn what grips are best for you. Just remember to always have your two main fingers on top and your thumb under the ball.

I didn't realize the different ways to hold the ball until I was in professional baseball. I then established a sinking fastball along with one that would tail in to a right-handed hitter. Without being aware of it, I found that I was tucking my thumb under the ball, and it was coming out of my hand differently. This pressure on the ball from below was causing the ball to rotate downward, and the ball began to sink.

Arm Action

The most important aspect of pitching is your arm action. Arm action is the path that your throwing arm takes as you take the ball behind your back to throw. Your path should be a circle. The throwing hand should drop back behind you as you start to throw and continue in a circle as you bring the ball up to throw. The better circle you make behind you the better your pitches will be, and the healthier your arm will be.

As you make the circle behind you, the bend to your elbow should be almost an L. The bend should stay at about an 80-degree angle until you get fully extended back toward centerfield. The wrist should not be bent at all as you take it back behind you. Then, as your arm starts forward, your arm straightens out, and your wrist will actually wrap back slightly before the ball is released.

Figure 2-5. Alex Fernandez shows the L bend to the elbow with his fingers on top of the ball and the proper extension behind his body.

You should not take the ball out of your glove straight down to the ground or straight back. Let your throwing arm naturally drop behind you and make a circle with your hand. If your path has straight extension down or back or if you pull the ball straight up behind you as you throw, you have improper arm action. A later chapter in this book includes a great drill that is designed to help your arm action.

Do not curl your wrist or your arm behind your body as you start to throw. Wrapping your wrist or curling your arm will cause many problems in the future, both with your pitching and with the health of your arm. Let your throwing arm flow freely behind you in a circular motion and show the ball to the centerfielder as you go. This sequence is the proper arm action.

Pitchers who do not have a circle behind them risk injury. This risk exists because if the arm straightens out in a stab behind the back, it must come out of that position with the bend of the elbow before you deliver the ball to the plate. If your body gets ahead of the arm, the arm must quicken to catch up to the body. This factor will cause quick flexion of the elbow and will place considerable stress on the tendons and muscles of the elbow.

Figure 2-6. This photo illustrates a wrist wrap. This locks the wrist immediately as you take the ball behind you and prohibits quick movement to the pitch.

If you curl the wrist during your take back, the wrist must unwrap to deliver the pitch. Because the arm uses its energy unwrapping the wrist, you lose the flexion of the wrist at release necessary to create tight spin to the ball. This factor is why wrappers have straighter fastballs and slower breaking curveballs and sliders. Wrappers do not risk injury as much as they lose their effectiveness pitching. Wrappers must stay back longer over the rubber to allow their arm to catch up and make effective pitches.

Figure 2-7. This picture shows how the wrist is still wrapped as the pticher has started to the plate. He has very little time for his wrist to uncurl before the ball is released. His arm will be late and the extension of the wrist, hand, and fingers to create spin to the pitch will be very difficult to achieve.

Pitching from the Stretch

Like any athletic move, the act of pitching a baseball is a combination of balance and power. In either the windup or the set position, you should try to get in a tall, balanced position over the rubber so that you can make a powerful, controlled move toward the plate while keeping the downward plane.

You should start at the beginning of the delivery from a set or stretch position. The set position is where you would set up if a man is on base, and you must hold him close to keep him from stealing the next base. It is easier to picture and practice these teachings from a set position and then incorporate them into your windup at a later time. The windup is the motion you use when nobody is on base.

Most pitchers will stand on the armside of the rubber. That is the right side of the rubber for a right-handed pitcher and the left side for a left-handed pitcher. This positioning is meant to create a better angle to the plate so that the ball comes from the pitcher's hand from more of a side angle, rather than straight into the batter.

It is not essential to pitch from this side of the rubber, but it will force you to finish your delivery properly to get the ball to the opposite side of the plate. You may find over time that you would prefer to be in the middle of the rubber, but it is suggested that you begin your delivery from the same side of the rubber as your arm.

While holding the ball with the armside foot on the rubber or in the hole in front of the rubber, you can stand balanced with your weight on your rubber foot. It is easier to square your body to the base you are facing (third base for a right-hander and first base for a left-hander). From a relaxed position, you look in for the sign from the

Figure 2-8. Jack McDowell looks in for the sign from a set position. He is square to third base and is in a comfortable, balanced position.

catcher and then raise your front foot and plant it under your front shoulder in a balanced position. Your hands should stop in a comfortable spot, normally about chest high.

If you rest your hands too low, for example at the belt level, it will be necessary to bring them back up to your shoulders to throw the ball. This movement is unnecessary. If you rest your hands too high, for example at the forehead level, you will have a tendency to pull the throwing arm straight back on a line rather than the proper arm arc of down to the belt and make a circle behind you.

At this point, you should be in a comfortable, standing position with your shoulders even and your hands relaxed in front of you. Your feet should be under your shoulders and square to the base. Crouching or bending will put you in a coiled position, and you would have to come out of that curl and spin somewhat during your delivery to the plate. It is recommended that you try to stand as relaxed as possible in the set position. Your shoulders should be even parallel to the ground. Your elbows should point to the ground below your glove.

As you start to the plate, remember the following key points. You should maintain your balance over the rubber until you begin your movement to the plate. This factor will allow you good direction, straight to the catcher and to your intended target. This balance over the rubber is essential to controlling your movements to the plate, and this alone will greatly improve your control and location of the pitch. The more unnecessary moves you make with your body, the greater the possibility of throwing off your direction and thus diminishing your ability to control the pitch.

It is important that your lead foot, when lifted, stay underneath your knee. One good reminder of how to do this is to lift your leg with your *thigh* rather than your foot.

If you use your foot to begin the lift, the tendency will be to kick your foot outward and thus lose some of your body control. Kicking your foot out can also make your shoulders go back in an arch position and alter the direction to the plate.

Figure 2-9. Greg Maddux is in a perfect balanced position. His foot is under his knee, his hands are in front of his chest, and his back leg is tall. This is the position you should attempt to be in.

Keeping your lead leg under control is extremely important in keeping balance and direction to the target. Swinging your leg back behind the rubber and behind your body may make you feel more powerful and may result in more velocity at times, but it will also make you lose control.

Figure 2-10. Dwight Gooden of the New York Mets shows a perfect balanced position. His lead foot is under his knee. His back leg is tall, and his hands are in front of his face. Try to reach this position out of the windup or the stretch.

As you bring your lead leg up to begin the delivery, you should keep your back leg tall until you separate your hands. This will keep you *tall* and maintain your proper plane. Your hands separate as you take the ball back in an arc behind your back toward centerfield, and your lead or glove arm should be kept at a relaxed position in front of your chest or face. This will enable you to maintain your angle to the plate, keep your body closed and back over the rubber, and allow you to make one power move to the plate.

Figure 2-11. Roger Clemens reaches the same balance point with his hands slightly lower than Gooden's. Notice the power he will be able to generate to the plate with his legs from this position.

As you take the ball back, your lead elbow should remain at shoulder height or slightly above. Your glove should be below your lead elbow and facing open to the ground or curled toward your chest. This inversion of your lead arm will keep you tall and maintain your downward plane. As you then drive to the plate, your lead shoulder will drive down toward the ground, and your elbow will follow.

Figure 2-12. Clemens shows the ball to the center fielder, illustrating the correct arm arc. The lead elbow is inverted face-high. This keeps the lead shoulder closed in order to drive down to his landing leg and extend to the target.

Figure 2-13. The lead elbow is above the lead shoulder, and the glove is just below the elbow. This positioning will keep you high to throw on a downward plane.

Figure 2-14. As his lead elbow drives to the target, his glove flips up to his body as he drives to his front leg.

As your elbow drives down, the glove will naturally open up to the sky or fall off to your side as you drive down over a bent front leg. Your glove hand keeps your lead shoulder closed long enough to make the proper move to the plate. Keeping your glove close to your body and under control will greatly help you have one compact, powerful move to the plate.

Your throwing hand extends toward your landing foot. Your front arm should stay close enough to your body to maintain your power and direction. Because your throwing arm will take the same path as your glove arm, it is important to take your lead arm the same direction as your natural throwing angle.

As you drive to your landing foot, you should feel that all of your power is directed from top to bottom. Your landing foot will absorb your energy and direction if you have maintained your downward plane. You can throw with maximum arm speed through your landing foot and maintain control of your pitches if your balance is good throughout your delivery.

Figure 2-15. As Roger Clemens drives over his landing leg, his lead shoulder is still closed and able to lead his throwing arm downhill to the plate.

Figure 2-16. Mark Buehrle maintains control of his finish by keeping his glove close to his body.

When your lead foot lands it should be at a slightly closed position to the hitter. For a right-handed pitcher, the foot should point to the right-hand batter's box. Opening your foot to point straight to the plate or even to the left-hand batter's box will open your shoulders and also take away the resistance on your landing foot at release. Your landing foot is the lever you use to throw against and extend over. This closing of your landing foot is vital to many things that will be discussed later in this book.

If you could draw a line from the tip of your back foot to the tip of your landing foot, this line extended would touch the plate. This is known as a toe-to-toe landing. If you can perfect this landing, your direction will always be good to the target, and more importantly it will help the health of your arm.

Figure 2-17. Roger Clemens is one of the best at driving down over the leg. Even this still picture illustrates how he drives downward and his landing leg absorbs the power.

When you land, your chest should be over your landing knee. This positioning will allow you to extend down toward the ground and finish properly. If your chest is behind your landing knee, your stride is too far. You will then lose angle and tend to push the ball to the plate. Your chest should stay over your knee as you extend your throwing arm.

Figure 2-18. Greg Maddux shows the proper toe-to-toe landing, with his front foot slightly closed at impact.

As your foot lands, simply extend your index and middle fingers down to your landing foot as the ball leaves your hand. Your throwing hand should continue outside your landing knee and complete your finish. Do not stop your arm once the ball leaves your hand. Let it decelerate on its own as it goes around your knee.

Figure 2-19. This side view of the finish shows how Greg Maddux gets his chest over his bent front leg. He controls his landing and is able to drive the ball directly to the catcher's mitt.

The aforementioned factors are the keys to a consistent delivery. As you will see, these factors are paramount to your ability to throw curveballs, sliders, change-ups, sinkers, or any other pitch you may attempt.

Figure 2-20. Roger Clemens extends his hand to his landing foot, as his leg begins to straighten.

Figure 2-21. Mark Buehrle continues around his landing knee, as he allows his throwing arm to decelerate gradually and naturally.

Figure 2-22. Tom Seaver finishes throwing a breaking ball, with his hand almost touching the ground to achieve full extension.

Figure 2-23. This picture shows Richard Dotson when he pitched for the White Sox. In the left most image, he is balanced and looking in for the sign from the stretch position. In the middle frame, he reaches a balanced, set position with his hands in front of his stomach. In the right frame, he finishes his delivery with his front leg bent and his glove under control. His fingers are on top of the ball and his head is on the target.

The most effective way to create any kind of movement on a fastball is to finish properly. The resistance that your landing leg creates is paramount to the amount of spin you can create. Pitchers who land on a stiff front leg do not allow themselves to extend over that leg and thus cut down on the driving of the ball on the downward plane to the plate. These pitchers appear to have a standup delivery and often spin sideways from their intended target. However, if you can get over a bent front leg, you can indeed drive down toward the target, get extension over that leg, and thus create maximum velocity and spin. Your landing leg should act as a cushion with resistance as you complete your pitch. You should extend your fingers and hand against and through your landing leg.

This finish is imperative to both spinning the ball and controlling the ball in the strike zone. You will still be balanced at the finish while getting maximum extension in a natural way. You will be square to the plate and also be in a great fielding position. As a matter of fact, if you are in a solid fielding position, you have probably done things right throughout your delivery.

Figure 2-24. The resistance created by Mark Buehrle with this landing allows him to spin the ball properly for any of his pitches.

Figure 2-25. His landing leg acts as a cushion for him to drive his pitches over with power and control.

As your lead foot lands and you drive the ball to the plate, you direct all of your power to the ground. This is the only resistance you have to work against. This resistance allows you to power the ball to the plate and create spin to the ball. Driving through your landing foot to the ground allows you to create maximum arm speed and maximum velocity. The pitcher who lands on a stiff landing leg extends his effort to the side, rather than into the ground. Creating any depth to the movement of the pitch is very difficult unless you can drive down onto your landing leg.

The Windup

As you begin to incorporate this movement into a windup, the mechanics are the same. After you take your step back and then lift your lead leg and bring your hands to your chest, you want to get into the balanced relaxed position you were in at the set position.

You will bring up your knee with your thigh muscles and keep your foot under your knee. Stay tall on your back leg until you break your hands. Reach the balance point over the rubber with your lead leg under control just as you did in the set position. Then all the principles of the delivery remain the same as you move to the plate.

Figure 2-26. Pedro Martinez is in a balanced, relaxed position as he looks in for the sign to begin his windup.

Figure 2-27. Pedro Martinez reaches the same tall, balanced position with every delivery. As a result, he has greater control of his pitches.

Remember to keep your leg swing to a minimum, with your front leg under control to reach balance. Because you are stepping into the rubber out of the windup, there will be a tendency to kick out your lead foot. Pick up your lead foot with your thigh and not your foot and keep your foot under your knee. Get to your balance point, and simply break your hands and drive down to your target.

Some pitchers like to bring their hands over their head in the windup, and some prefer to just rotate with their hands in front of their chest. Either way is fine as long as you remain under control. You might want to take your hands over your head if you can keep your balance. This step gets your arms moving and relaxes them in the delivery. You will feel stronger yet under control.

This disciplined approach is intended to minimize the effort needed to pitch and to maximize your power and control. You will free your throwing arm to make an arc behind you as you prepare to deliver the ball to the plate.

Figure 2-28. Richard Dotson goes over his head in his windup and maintains control of his body as he lifts his hands.

Figure 2-29. Hall of Fame pitcher Steve Carlton turns his foot into the front of the rubber as his hands go over his head to begin the windup.

Figure 2-30. This sequence of Richard Dotson's windup shows how he gets from set up to finish. He makes no unnecessary movements, and all of his actions are directed to get to balance and finish.

Moving Late

One of the major components of being a successful pitcher is the ability to make the ball move just before it reaches the plate. To accomplish this consistently and effectively, your throwing arm *path* must make a circle in the back of your delivery, and you must get extension over your landing leg at completion. The circle should be full but not too long in the arm swing where your arm is fully extended. A very long arm swing will diminish the velocity and the spin and thus deter the movement on the ball.

Your elbow should be just above your shoulder of the throwing arm throughout the throw. Your hand should be above your elbow. If your release point and elbow get too low, you will sling the ball rather than throw it. Throwing with a lower elbow may be effective later in life, but you should avoid throwing with a low elbow while you are developing. Throwing with your hand even with or below your elbow will cause you to get around the side of the ball and turn your wrist. Either one of these improper mechanics can lead to elbow soreness.

Figure 2-31. This photo illustrates a high, three-quarter delivery with the hand above the elbow and the elbow above the shoulder. The landing is toe-to-toe and the landing foot slightly closed.

Movement on a pitch can be described as the distance in the change of direction the ball makes as it nears the plate. In a baseball sense, the definition of "life" is the quickness with which the ball moves. For example, if you throw a fastball that sinks about six inches, you would have good movement to the pitch. If the fastball sinks only four inches but does not sink until it is five feet from the plate, you would have good life to your fastball. A big curveball that breaks down 12 inches would be a good pitch because of the amount of movement. If you throw a curveball that may break only six inches but has a sharp late break that occurs just as it nears the plate, you have a very good pitch. If it breaks 12 inches and breaks very late, then you have a great pitch.

A batter can adjust to a big break as he gets experience and improves. This adjustment takes quite a bit of experience. Most hitters who come into the minor leagues do not handle breaking pitches very well. Over the next two to three years of their career, they learn how to make this adjustment.

The best movement a pitch can have is the changing of planes. It is very rare to see a pitcher who can make the ball rise. This attribute is a natural talent that most players do not possess.

With the proper techniques, you can make the ball sink. All of the pitches you will learn have the ability to sink. Maintaining the downward plane is the main essential to causing the ball to go down as it nears the plate. The resistance created in the landing is the other vital essential in this pursuit. The quicker and later you can make the ball sink determines much of your success of a pitcher. No matter what pitch you throw, the hitter will have a hard time adjusting to the movement of the pitch if the ball dives downward as it nears the plate. The mechanics of the delivery explained in this book are essential to creating consistent late movement and drop to your pitches.

The late sharp-breaking curveball or slider is a pitch that hitters do not see very often and is more challenging to hit hard because of the time factor. If the ball breaks late as it nears the plate, the hitter doesn't have time to adjust his swing to center the ball on the bat. He gauges where the ball will be as it crosses the plate and swings the bat to that place based on his experience. Movement to the pitch greatly depends on your ability to land slightly closed over your front leg. The resistance you create from your landing leg allows you to extend your arm over your landing foot and as your fingers leave the ball it creates the spin to make the ball move or break. You will feel the spin that you create when you do this properly. As you get older and stronger, the speed with which your arm travels will increase. As your arm speed increases, the spin of the ball will increase and improve the movement and life to your pitches.

Any pitch can have life. Most often people refer to life on your fastball. Again, it is because you have the arm speed, stay back long enough to allow your arm to catch up, stay tall in your delivery, and finish over your soft or bent front leg. You will have confidence in not only the pitch but also in your ability to throw it over the plate. This confidence will breed firmness in your delivery. You can throw the ball through the glove rather than to it, and life will occur.

This life is the common attribute for successful Major League pitchers. They can throw the ball with confidence and determination. As they extend over their front leg, the fastball can *take off* in the direction that is natural for them. Whether the ball sinks or tails or rises or cuts, it is this drive through the throwing motion that gives them life.

Some pitchers can actually make the ball appear to rise as it nears the plate. Most experts believe that this is only an optical illusion—it appears the ball is rising, but it actually is simply riding to the armside. This movement or appearance of movement can only be achieved with great arm strength and a very free delivery. (This is a natural talent, and I have never seen anyone work to establish this skill.) However, the only way to show this skill is with the delivery you are striving to master. Life on a pitch is even more effective than movement. You will see a lot of check swings when your pitches have life.

There probably won't be a major change to the movement of your pitches until your hands are fully developed. Be patient and let nature take its course. But when you are at high school age, you can begin to practice different grips along with grip pressure. This step can make your practice sessions more fun and enlightening.

As your body grows and your hands get bigger, you will naturally improve. Your fingers will get longer and your body taller, and you simply need to work on the delivery to get the most out of your ability.

The movement of the ball or an altering of the ball's course to the plate is determined by three factors:

- Take the ball freely from your glove without any wrapping of your wrist or stabbing the ball out from your body. Make a circle behind you during your arm swing. This will allow freedom of your fingers and wrist to extend at the finish and cause spin to the ball.
- Finish your delivery correctly with extension over your soft bent front leg with your foot slightly closed to the plate. Use your soft landing leg as a lever to extend over with your throwing hand.
- Be aware of the pressure points of your grip and how the ball leaves your hand.

The pre-high school age pitcher should spend his efforts on the mechanics of throwing and developing the extension over his front leg for the fastball and watch the ball for spin and movement. The catcher can tell you what type of spin the ball naturally has.

Normally, the ball will have a tailing spin to the armside or some sinking spin. Tailing spin means the ball will move to the same side as your arm. For a right-handed thrower, it will tail to the right side before it reaches your receiver. If this is not the case for you, then you do not have your fingers properly on top of the ball. If your elbow drops and/or your fingers slide to the side of the ball, the ball will spin in the opposite or cutting direction. This occurrence is a sign of improper throwing motion and will cause you to have elbow problems over time.

You can learn a lot before high school in recognizing the spin of the ball after it leaves your hand when throwing a fastball. Practice different grips with the fastball with your fingers together or some separation to your top two fingers. Remember to feel the ball leave your fingertips and drive those fingers down over the landing leg. Recognize what effect your thumb has when placed below or to the side of the ball. *Make a circle behind you with the ball, achieve a power move to the plate while maintaining control throughout, and land over your bent landing leg. Recognize how different grips on the ball and how you land affects the movement of your pitches.*

3

Delivery Flaws and Staying Healthy

The delivery mechanics described in Chapter 2 can also help keep you from hurting your arm. If you maintain balance and have a good arc to your throwing arm, you can throw more often and more effectively. There will be no strain on any part of your arm. You will be able to compete with all of your pitches without fear of hurting yourself.

Out of the three most common ways to hurt your arm, losing balance and rushing to the plate is the most common. This situation occurs when the pitcher gets quick during his delivery and *rushes* to the plate. The body gets ahead of the throwing arm, and the arm is constantly trying to catch up to the rest of his body.

Throughout the 1990s, the Chicago White Sox filmed the top pitchers in the country for the draft, and they found that about 80 percent of the amateur pitchers in the United States had this common problem. A pitcher with this problems feels as if he is really powering the ball with a lot of effort. The reality is that his velocity does not increase, and his control and the downward plane are lost.

Rushing also affects the movement of the ball, elevating the ball in the strike zone rather than driving the ball down through the lower portion. This elevation of the ball occurs because the arm doesn't catch up to the body. The ball leaves the hand before the pitcher gets over the landing leg. The closer the ball is to the hitter's eyes, the easier it is for him to make good contact. Squatting on your back leg as soon as you start your move to the plate usually causes rushing. You not only lose your downward plane, but you also throw out your lead shoulder.

Remember that no time clock exists in baseball, and staying over the rubber during your delivery will keep you balanced and powerful. When a pitcher rushes, he has to make a lot of adjustments along the way to throw strikes. In the process, he cannot maintain direction or provide proper finish to add spin to the ball.

The second most common way to hurt your arm is not making the proper arc. The curling of your arm as you separate your hand from your glove or wrapping your wrist during the process has many effects. First and foremost, you put your arm in an unnatural position and do not allow full extension. Arm curling or *hookers,* as they are called in baseball, often develop elbow problems over time. These problems result from the pressure they put on their joints by being coiled with their arm back during extension. They must then uncoil their arm as they make their arc behind them before they throw the ball. Then, at release, they have to bend the joints again to throw. If their timing is wrong and they have to hurry through this process, they put great stress on their joints and can develop shoulder, or more commonly, elbow problems.

If you have a wrist wrap during the delivery, you must come out of the wrap position before the ball leaves your hand. You cannot extend your fingers through the release and cause the ball to spin with any sharp rotation.

Wrappers, as they are called in baseball, have a propensity for straighter fastballs and very slow breaking balls that tend to roll to the plate rather than drop sharply. Remember that you are trying to get the ball to move as close to the plate as possible, giving the hitter less time to react to the change of direction. The later and the sharper you make the ball move, the less chance the hitter has to hit the ball solidly.

It is important to not stab the ball back in a straight line behind you as you separate your throwing arm from your glove. If you pull the ball straight back at shoulder height or straight to the ground, you will be unable to make the proper circle in the back. As a result, your pitches will lack life, and you may experience arm problems later on.

The third common way to hurt your arm is landing stiff on your front leg. Landing stiff does not allow your throwing arm to decelerate properly, and you will cut off your finish. Accordingly, it is vital that your mechanics are controlled to allow you to land over a slightly bent front leg and extend through at the finish. If you can repeat the same proper delivery, you will have very little chance for injury and will be able to throw all of your pitches effectively and with control.

Most shoulder injuries are caused by the improper deceleration of the arm at the finish. It is vitally important to extend through and finish properly. Pitchers who stop their arm quickly after releasing the pitch are susceptible to shoulder injuries. Landing stiff will tend to make you want to stop your arm too quickly because you have a feel of losing your balance at the landing point.

Some pitchers will actually recoil at the finish. In other words, they stop or even pull their throwing arm back as they finish. Sometimes, they will even pull back their throwing shoulder after releasing the pitch. Pitchers who recoil are at great risk for incurring a shoulder injury. This is why the landing is emphasized so strongly.

Elbow trouble occurs if you turn your tendons and muscles in your throwing arm laterally or sideways. These musculoskeletal units were not meant to be turned

Figure 3-1. Dwight Gooden finishes this curveball with his hand going around his knee. He allows his throwing arm to naturally decelerate, which is a great finish to the curveball.

sideways or in a spinning direction. They should be extended down and through when you finish your delivery.

You can feel these tendons with one simple test. Place your fingers of your non-throwing hand on the inside of your elbow just above the bone. Duplicate the throwing of a fastball with your fingers going downward toward the ground. You should feel very little movement to the tendons in your elbow. At this point, turn your throwing wrist as if you were trying to spin the ball sideways with your thumb moving up and your little finger moving down. You can then feel, with your fingers, that the tendons in your elbow are turning.

This twisting of your tendons is what causes soreness and ultimately injury if constantly repeated. This is the incorrect way to release the ball. Throwing with a low elbow or turning the ball to make it break sideways will cause you to throw improperly.

Practice throwing the ball with the index and middle fingers on top of the ball and extend them straight toward the ground at release. This should make the ball tail naturally as your hand comes off the ball. This is the proper extension at release. It is important to be aware of your own physical changes when you go through these stages of development.

Some pitchers tend to *push* the ball to the plate. Pushing the ball is a result of leading your throwing arm motion with the elbow. If your elbow gets ahead of the ball hand, you will drop your elbow to allow the throwing hand to come through.

Pushing the ball to the plate will result in a flat throw that cannot change planes. It can also result in soreness from the turning of your elbow that results after your hand comes through. If you find yourself pushing the ball, use the long-toss program illustrated in Chapter 4 to reinforce the correct method of throwing.

Figure 3-2. This sequence of pictures shows the proper arm circle. Alex Fernandez takes the ball out of the glove with an L bend to his elbow. As he draws it back, his arm begins to extend with his fingers on top of the ball. His hand comes up, and he begins to show the ball to the centerfielder.

When you are on the mound, you sometimes will attempt to make each pitch the very best you have ever thrown. When you do throw a fastball by the hitter, you sometimes will attempt to throw the next one even harder. It is important to recognize what abilities you have and try to stay within yourself and not try to do something with the ball that you are not capable of doing. This situation is a common dilemma for all pitchers despite their experience. The more you understand your own limitations, the better you can perform.

To this point, this book has tried to cover releases and grips for the benefit of all readers, regardless of their age. In this regard, one major fear is that you may try to incorporate some of the aforementioned suggestions into your pitching repertoire before you are physically ready. Talk to your coaches or parents before you attempt something new. If you are unsure, wait until you know you are able to handle the demands that will be imposed by the effort.

If at any point you experience pain or soreness in any part of your arm, *stop*. If you continue, you can cause irreparable harm and may never reach your potential. You should always report any arm soreness to your coach or doctor. Being a hero for a day is not worth the price you will pay with your future. *Always keep a fluid arc with an L bend to your elbow around to extension, and stay over the rubber until you can make one power move to the plate.*

4

How Should You Practice?

Many coaches and young pitchers often ask what a youngster can do to develop pitching skills. The number one thing that you should do is to throw. The more you just play catch, the better shape your arm gets in for throwing.

The arc that the arm makes is crucial to the development of a pitcher in many ways. The arc behind should be circular and full although it should not be with an arm fully extended. There should be some bend in the elbow. The throwing hand should always be above the elbow. The best practice for the correct arm arc is known as the long toss. As you are playing catch to loosen up, you should constantly keep moving back away from your throwing partner as you feel your arm get loose. You should gradually go back to a distance where you can still throw the ball on a line and not have to arc the ball to get it to your partner.

Remember to release the ball from a high, three-quarter release point or almost overhand. Incorporate a hop with your feet or crow hop, as it is called, as if you were an outfielder throwing the ball to a base. Shuffle your feet toward your target as you get set to throw. It is important to use your legs in the long toss to generate power and free your arm to extend, and then to throw the ball firmly on a line.

The *crow hop* will cause your entire body to move toward the target with power and direction. You need to get good extension with your arm and feel as if you were reaching high up to get maximum velocity. Your middle and index fingers should be on top of the ball and across the seams of the baseball as you extend over your landing leg toward the target.

Practicing the long toss drill will illustrate the proper arm arc. When you are at maximum distance to throw a line drive to your partner, your arm will naturally make the correct arc for throwing. This drill not only helps to teach you the correct arc, it also helps to build up your arm strength to throw harder and teaches you how to keep your body under control, while using all of your effort to get the ball to your partner. This drill is the best exercise you can do on those days you are not pitching or to loosen up your arm before you throw on those days you are scheduled to pitch.

Your coach should watch the position of your arm to learn your natural release point. It may be almost overhand or a three-quarters release. You should make note of this and try to duplicate it in your pitching delivery. As you take the ball back, get in the practice of showing the ball to the centerfielder, and make a circle behind you as you throw. This step reinforces is the proper arc and hand position when pitching.

Figure 4-1. My son, Grant Monroe, begins the long toss drill by getting his feet below him.

Figure 4-2. He turns his body to begin the drill and firmly plants his right foot as he steps into the throw.

Figure 4-3. As his left foot lands, he hops his back foot up to gain momentum to his target.

Figure 4-4. When his right foot lands, he draws his arm back and begins to extend his left leg for maximum effort.

Figure 4-5. He begins to bring his throwing hand forward, as he drives to his left foot and begins to clear his front shoulder.

Figure 4-6. His throwing arm is reaching up to almost an overhand throwing motion, as his left foot cushions his landing.

Figure 4-7. He then extends his throwing arm over his landing leg, while maintaining his direction to the target. This drill is designed to teach you the correct arm path as you learn to pitch and to increase your arm strength over time.

If you repeat the arc used in long toss and show the ball back when you pitch, you will know that your hand and the ball are in the proper position to pitch. Showing the ball to the centerfielder will help eliminate any wrap or curl of your wrist and help ensure proper movement and a healthy throwing arm.

The major pitfall of not regularly practicing the aforementioned long toss program will be that you throw short distances and, as a result, will get in the habit of target throwing to the receiver, rather than making the full arc behind you and letting the ball go. If you need to arc the ball to get it to the receiver, then the distance is too far. If you engage in the long toss drill on a regular basis during the throwing season for a period of years, the effort will enhance your level of arm strength and allow you to develop naturally. As such, the drill will help with the development and strength of your throwing arm.

Pitching is *not* target practice! You should constantly throw the ball *through* the glove rather than *to* the glove. Understanding and adhering to this concept will help greatly when you are on the mound pitching. If you are having trouble understanding the delivery, practicing the long toss can be the best teacher. Go back to long toss anytime you are having mechanical problems.

It cannot be stressed enough that, especially in the formative years, the circle your arm makes while throwing should not be too short or too long. Taking the ball back short in the arm swing behind your body will lessen your arm strength and get you in the mode of target practice. In turn, this action will diminish your ability to spin the ball with the fastball or breaking balls and may also lead to arm problems.

The long toss exercise will also keep you from having too long of an arc behind you. When throwing the ball, it is proper to have a bend in your elbow, with your elbow above your shoulder and your hand above the elbow. Always remember that it is imperative that you not curl your wrist in any way when taking the ball down and back through the backside arc. It is best to make a circle behind your back, and show the ball to the centerfielder during the motion. The throwing hand should have continuous motion and *never* stop during the throwing process.

Your practice sessions on the mound should be geared toward recognizing what you do well and the things you don't do well. Most pitchers control their fastball better on the armside of the plate rather than the other side; i.e., a right-handed pitcher is more skilled at throwing to the inside part of the plate to a right-handed hitter than to the outside portion of the plate.

If this is indeed true for you, it is better to practice throwing the majority of your fastballs to the outside part of the plate. In time, you will gain confidence to throwing to your weaker side. Remember to always throw *through* the glove and not *to* the glove.

When you are working from the mound, practice adhering to the correct mechanics and extending over your landing leg to get the ball to the outside. When you can consistently get the ball to that part of the plate, while maintaining your proper delivery, you will be well on your way to being successful.

You can also work on your delivery without throwing a ball. Stand in front of a mirror at home and watch what your hands and feet are doing when you go through your delivery. When you reach the balanced position, is your lead foot swinging out, or are you keeping it under your knee? Does your arm swing make a circle in the back? Are you cocking your wrist in a curled position behind your back? These are the common mistakes that looking at yourself in the mirror will help you recognize.

Another way that you can recognize delivery flaws is simply to watch others pitch. Since at this point you understand the elements of a proper delivery, you will see others make some of the common mistakes that have been reviewed in this book. You will probably see first that others have the tendency to rush through their delivery and not get balanced over the rubber. Their arm will be late and then speed up to catch up to their bodies. They will not finish properly, and some may spin off at the finish. Their pitches will tend to be up and out of the strike zone. They will not be able to get the ball to the farther side of the plate (i.e., right-hand pitchers won't be able to get the ball away from a right-hand hitter for a strike). They may also tend to land on a stiff front leg. Pitchers who rush will land stiff to stop their momentum and keep from falling.

If pitchers curl their wrist or wrap the ball behind them, their arm will also tend to be late, and they too will leave the pitch up. Their fastball will be unable to change planes up or down. Their breaking ball will tend to have a slow spin and not break sharply but rather roll to the plate. This result will also occur if the pitcher lacks sufficient arm extension behind him or *short-arms* the ball. He will give no crisp spin to the ball.

The pitcher may tend to break down his back leg or sit over the rubber. You will be able to see how he loses his downward plane and appears as if he is pushing the ball to the plate. The result is a lack of depth to his pitches.

A fine line exists between good and bad deliveries. Over time, however, you will recognize the lack of consistency in the performance of those pitchers who make these common mistakes. Your muscle memory will try to take over and compensate for these flaws, but eventually it will become natural for you to throw in this incorrect way. It is important to be able to see these flaws and correct them before they become a habit that will be very hard to fix later.

If you have trouble pitching to both sides of the plate, you should try to film or video yourself pitching, as it is evident that some part of your mechanics is breaking down. Are you rushing through your delivery? Is your landing toe-to-toe? Is your direction to the catcher off to one side or the other? You could be breaking down your back leg too early and pushing the ball to the plate. You may be dropping your arm down toward a sidearm angle and getting around the ball.

The use of videotapes when analyzing your delivery is always helpful. You will be able to see if you are doing all of the proper things correctly. Major League baseball teams have used tapes of their pitchers as a terrific teaching tool, and since many of you have access to a camcorder, you can do the same thing. It can help you to better understand the entire delivery. Coaches use these videotapes to make necessary corrections in their pitchers. In time, you should be able to recognize when you lose control and should, in those instances, be able to make the proper adjustment.

The aforementioned are the trouble points that you will be able to see on the tape or, better yet, feel them as you deliver the pitch. When you reach the point where you can feel things in your delivery, you will be *well* on your way to being very successful. If you can feel, for instance, that you are rushing your delivery and then see that the ball seems to be high and to the armside, you can make the necessary adjustment. The ability to use the information presented in this book to correct your delivery will help to give you a tremendous push toward achieving consistency.

Pitching is unique in that you cannot throw all day working on those things that need improvement. Because you can only throw so much on any given day, it is imperative that you use your time to work on those factors that you do not do well. If you can develop the delivery shown in this book, you will be able to throw the ball to both sides of the plate. *Practice the long toss drill often to learn the proper mechanics for you throwing. The more you throw properly, the quicker you will improve.*

5

The Pitcher's Repertoire

This chapter looks at the various pitches available in the pitcher's battle against the hitter. It is important to remember that the pitches you employ depend upon your age and arm development. Hopefully, the information presented in this chapter can be stored in your memory back until it can be used in an appropriate manner and at an appropriate time.

From years of scouting, it has been found that the best and most effective pitchers have one common trait that relates to pitches other than the fastball. They will throw their slider seven miles per hour slower than their fastball. Their curveball will be 12 miles per hour slower than their fastball, and those with the best change-ups will throw this particular pitch approximately 10 to 15 miles per hour slower than their fastball.

While the aforementioned velocities may vary one to two mph, the most successful pitchers stay in this range to maintain an appropriate level of deception and movement of the pitch. This velocity checklist can be a great learning tool for coaches and pitchers as you practice spinning the slider or curveball. This speed check alone can determine if any wrist wrap or slowing of the arm occurs during delivery.

The Fastball

The basic fastball that most pitchers throw is known as a four-seam fastball. This designation is based on the fact that your top two fingers cross over the four main seams of the ball. The seams fit under the first knuckle of your index and middle fingers, and you have a feeling of pulling down the ball at release. This fastball will tend to have some tail to it when thrown properly. It usually will not sink, however.

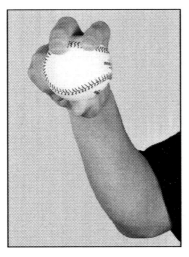

Figure 5-1. This photo shows a four-seam grip, with the index and middle fingers separated. Most youngsters tend to use this grip until they have the strength and hand size to bring their fingers together.

The other fastball that pitchers throw is known as a two-seam fastball, so named because your fingers are placed over the two seams of the ball that are closest together. You will still be on top of the ball at release, but the seams do not rotate from top to bottom but rather sideways. This action usually causes the ball to spin sideways with a tailing action, but the spin of the ball may cause it to sink. Sinkerball pitchers use this grip.

As you begin practicing, it is best to use the four-seam fastball. This pitch helps you stay on top of the ball and finish down and through the ball. When you have accomplished the proper delivery and throw the four-seam fastball, it will be easy to see the natural movement of your pitches. Over time, you can experiment with the grips you've learned in this book and see what type of life you can get to your fastball. When you reach high school, you can then try the two-seam fastball and see if the movement is different.

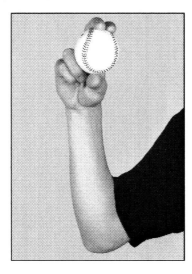

Figure 5-2. The two-seam grip places the fingers together over the two seams that are nearest together.

Having a command of your fastball is the *most* important thing you must accomplish to be a successful pitcher. It should be your number one goal. Practice this more than anything else until you are confident you can throw the fastball to an area of about a catcher's glove size. When you can do this without aiming the ball but simply because your mechanics are repeated, you have accomplished the most important goal of your pitching career. The rest will be relatively easy.

As you get older, you can begin to off-center the top of the ball. This step involves keeping your fingers on top of the ball and moving them off to one side of the ball, rather than directly on the top center of the ball. This positioning will usually cause the ball to have a sideways spin and break across one way or the other. When practicing this step, be sure to be on top of the ball. Do not get to the side and spin the ball. Get the feel of throwing the ball straight down, and the grip itself will make the ball move. You can also put your two fingers together when gripping the ball. The following checklist can help identify delivery problems that may exist when yor are throwing your fastball:

- Is your lead foot under your knee and under control throughout your delivery?

- Is your body twisting too far around the rubber as you take the ball back?

- Are you curling the ball in your back swing or wrapping your wrist?

- Are your head and back arching back and forcing you to pull off your pitches?

- Are you breaking down or bending your back leg too early before you have started forward, and therefore pushing the ball to the plate?

- Are you rushing to the plate and landing early so that your arm is constantly trying to catch up to your body?

- Are you landing toe-to-toe so that the points of your toes point to home plate?

- Is your landing foot in a slightly closed position rather than opening up your foot and body too much?

- Are you able to extend through over a bent front leg in a controlled landing while still driving the ball to the glove?

The Curveball

Most individuals believe that a curveball thrown by a right-hand pitcher will break away from the right-hand hitter. This belief is partly true. However, the most effective curveball you can throw is one that breaks straight down.

The ultimate goal for a curveball pitcher is to have a late, sharp break downward, changing planes so that the hitter must adjust. This curveball, when thrown properly, will be the toughest for the hitter to adjust to. It is also the easiest one to throw and is much easier on your throwing arm.

The proper curveball technique is to turn your hand just before delivering the ball to a sideways cocked position with your middle and index fingers *on top* of the ball and with your thumb under the ball. This technique enables you to spin the ball downward. Your middle finger will be the power finger and the force that pulls the ball down.

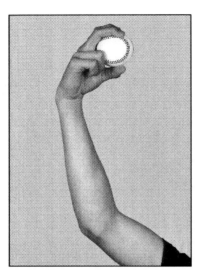

Figure 5-3. This photo illustrates the grip that has been found to be the most comfortable when learning the curveball. The middle finger has a long seam underneath it. The index finger is up against the middle finger. The thumb is under the ball and the hand is cocked. This grip allows you to feel the seam of the ball as you pull it down with your middle finger.

Figure 5-4. This photo shows Bert Blyleven who had one of the best curveballs of all time. Notice how his hand is in a sideways cocked position with his middle and index fingers on top of the ball.

Figure 5-5. Aaron Sele has the ball cocked for a curveball as he drives over his front leg.

One effective drill for working on the proper spin for a curveball is to get down on the floor on the same knee as your throwing arm. Cock the ball sideways and simply spin the ball into the floor and let it roll ten feet or so to a partner. As you watch the ball roll, you will recognize that if the ball veers off to the side you are turning the ball sideways at release. You want the ball to roll almost directly to your partner. The straighter the ball rolls without veering sideways, the more proper your technique is.

Although this drill will usually take two to three months to perfect on one knee, it will teach you the proper release for a curveball. Such a release will cause the ball to break in a downward direction rather than across. It is much tougher for a hitter to center the ball on the bat if the ball is changing planes or diving downward rather than just breaking across the strike zone.

Over time, you will be able to make the curveball break sharply down and also locate this pitch at about knee height. It is also by far the healthiest way to throw this pitch. Your tendons and muscles will elongate down toward your hand rather than turning sideways. Both the health of your arm and your ability to pitch will benefit.

You should not feel any turning of your elbow when practicing this technique. If you can feel your elbow turning, it is time to go back to one knee. Throwing a curveball by spinning the ball sideways is a dangerous thing to attempt.

The proper method of throwing the curveball should not be attempted until your high school years and only then if your body has developed enough. Even practicing throwing a curveball this correct way can be detrimental to your physical development if it is attempted too early in life.

The size of the break is not as important as the direction of the break. You will find as you begin to spin a curveball that it will have a gradual downward break. Over time, your arm speed will increase, and the break of the curveball should become smaller but tighter. Practice this grip and release to achieve the correct spin and the feel of pulling down with your middle finger. The correct delivery and increase in arm speed will sharpen your break, and the amount of the break will be natural and not forced. The quicker the ball moves downward, the better your curveball is.

At this point, as you begin to throw the curveball, refer back to the earlier information on grip and spin. When you then start spinning curveballs to a catcher, he can watch the spin and tell you if it is more downward than across. It is helpful to monitor this factor by imagining the hands on a clock. The top of the clock is 12 o'clock. For a right-handed pitcher, the high three-quarters part of the clock is 11 o'clock. For a left-handed pitcher, the high three-quarter side is 1 o'clock.

The catcher can see the direction from which the ball is spinning. This information gives the two of you a specific gauge so you can both understand the height from which your spin is coming. The ideal curveball should come from almost 12 o'clock. That would be a curveball that would break straight down. In reality, few individuals are able to achieve 12 o'clock. However, the closer you can get to 12 o'clock, the more effective you will be. The right-handed pitcher should try to stay between 12 and 11 o'clock. This positioning will ensure a downward break.

As you practice, you will discover that when you stay in this spin range and you begin to throw the curveball harder, the sharpness of the break will continue to increase. (A left-handed pitcher should attempt to stay between 12 and 1 o'clock.) When you are solid on your mechanics and achieve this direction on the clock, you will get a sharp downward break and great change of planes.

As you are warming up to practice your curveball, regardless if it is a game or simply practice, it is important to throw the first 10 to 15 pitches by simply spinning the ball to the catcher. It is best to have the catcher come in front of the plate and simply spin 10 or more pitches to get the proper release. You will then be able to get feedback from the catcher on the clock spin of the ball and, at the same time, loosen the muscles and tendons in your arm with this motion.

If you start by throwing the curveball too hard early in your warm-ups, you are vulnerable to injury. Starting at a shorter distance and simply spinning the ball will be very helpful. You can then gradually move back to the mound and make the last few throws from the rubber. At this point, you can gradually throw the curveball harder until you reach your maximum velocity.

Remember that the best curveball should break close to the plate and that the ideal location to work on is knee height. Don't be too concerned if the ball is inside or outside. If you can get the ball to end up with downward break and at the knees or below, you will have developed the ability to throw a good curveball.

Figure 5-6. This diagram uses the hands of the clock to illustrate the break of your pitch as the catcher sees it. If the ball breaks straight down, it is said to go 12 to 6 o'clock. The sharper and more downward you can cause the ball to break, the harder it is to hit. Many pitches, especially breaking balls—like curveballs and sliders, break from 11 to 5 o'clock or from 10 to 4 o'clock. The closer you can get to 12 to 6 o'clock with your curveball, the more successful you will be.

If your curveball tends to be too low and bounce on or near the plate, do not be concerned. All factors considered, this situation is a good thing, and you are throwing the ball correctly. The only corrections you need to make are simply changing the target you are focusing on and the time you are releasing the ball.

If you are looking at the catcher's glove as your target, you should instead throw at the catcher's mask. If the pitch then comes in too high, find a middle point between the glove and the mask to throw the ball to. It is much easier to adjust to throwing the curveball too low than it is if you are throwing it too high. The release should occur as you reach the highest point with your throwing hand while you simply pull it down over your landing leg.

When practicing the curveball, you should not force the ball to spin. Pull down easily with your middle finger to the ground and let the ball spin out. You can practice the release of the curveball by simply flicking a baseball up into the air while in a cocked position with your hand. Pull down with your middle finger and up with your thumb and spin it up in the air. As your release feels comfortable, you can throw the curveball with more force. The finish is the same for all pitches, and you can spin your curveball over a softly-bent front leg.

It is almost like snapping your fingers, but the ball is in between your thumb and middle finger. As you begin spinning your curveball, the release will become more natural.

As you increase your arm speed, the ball will spin tighter and create a sharper break. Getting the feel on how the ball comes out of your hand at the early point is more important than what the ball does. Duplicate the feel of the release in the kneel-down drill and let the ball roll off your middle finger. The downward sharpness will come.

Figure 5-7. Aaron Sele spins the curveball with his middle finger pulling down and the same proper finish as his other pitches.

The most common cause of leaving a curveball too high is rushing to the plate. The front part of your body is going to the plate before your arm can catch up. This action will leave the curveball up with loose spin and no sharp break. This pitch is known as a hanging curveball. A curveball up in the zone is one of the easiest pitches to hit. You must fix this problem if you want to keep this pitch in your repertoire.

If your curveball stays on the armside of the plate, you are releasing the ball too early. You should practice waiting until your arm reaches its highest point before releasing the ball. If the curveball goes to the far side of the plate, you are pulling your front shoulder open early and need to stay closed longer.

As you develop this pitch and continue to throw it, you will find that by focusing on the target, you can allow your mechanics to take over and throw the ball near the hitter's knees. As a rule, this skill will take time and repetition to develop, but eventually you will be amazed at how easy it is to throw this pitch around the knees with good break. Work on the spin and your delivery, and it will be able to throw a good pitch that puts little strain on your arm.

The Change-up

You can throw a change-up numerous ways. Pitchers tend to vary the degree to which they feel comfortable with the different grips and select one accordingly. When you find a comfortable grip, stay with it and learn how to decrease the velocity of the ball without slowing your arm motion. This skill can be difficult to master and will take time.

The most effective grips for a change-up are those held deep in the palm of your hand. You will most likely find that it is most comfortable having your index finger to the side of the ball rather than on top. Keep the ball deep in your hand and make sure that your other fingers are on top of the ball even if they aren't touching the ball.

Your index finger and middle finger are the power fingers when throwing the ball. Since you are attempting to decrease the velocity of the ball, you should not have the ball leave your hand with these fingers releasing the ball.

You can place your ring finger on top of the ball and even your middle finger. If your index finger is on the side of the ball, it will definitely decrease the velocity of the pitch. Whichever fingers are on the top of the ball, it is important to use them to throw the ball downward to the plate.

The best change-up is one that is not recognizable to the hitter in any way. The first factor to be aware of after you have found a grip you like is to make sure that you can decrease velocity without slowing the speed of your arm. A hitter will see when you slow your arm down and will be able to adjust early and get a good swing at the pitch.

Ideally, the spin of the ball on the change-up should be similar to, if not the same, as the spin to your fastball. Your catcher can help you with this factor by telling you if he can recognize a change-up either by the spin or the slowing of your arm. If he can recognize the pitch is a change-up by the spin of the ball, you should play with the grip of the ball with your fingers on top of the ball until it is comfortable. The spin of the fastball and change-up are similar.

You shouldn't get too comfortable with a change-up grip only to find out later in life that as the hitters get better, they too can recognize the pitch early after release. The time to make this adjustment is at the beginning of the process.

One very effective and comfortable change-up is simple to learn. If you make an okay sign with your fingers, you simply put the ball deep in your hand. Your index and little fingers are to the side of the ball, and your middle and ring fingers are on top of the ball. This pitch has become known as a *circle change-up* because your fingers form a circle around the ball.

At release, you should throw the ball with your two fingers on top of the ball and still extend down over your landing leg. This is how Pedro Martinez and many other pitchers throw an outstanding change-up. It will take some time for you to feel comfortable with this grip and release, but you will find that with practice, it is both effective and easy to control.

As you practice whichever change-up you choose to throw, you should focus on the two factors reviewed earlier. Hold the ball back in your hand with your middle and ring fingers above the ball and let your delivery take over. You will find that you will be

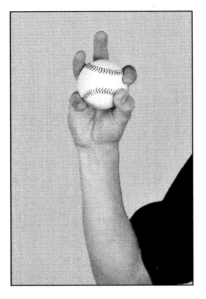

Figure 5-8. This photo illustrates the grip for the circle change-up. You make an okay sign with your fingers and then put the ball in the palm of your hand. Note that your thumb and index finger are on the inside of the ball and your little finger is to the outside. The ball will release from the base of your middle and ring fingers with these two fingers releasing from the top of the ball.

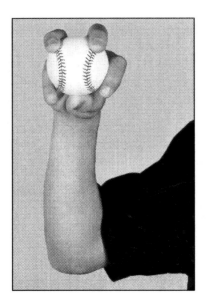

Figure 5-9. This photo shows the grip, used by some Major League pitchers, known as the fosh. The grip is similar to the circle change-up, but the middle and ring fingers are placed on top of the ball, and it is held deep in the palm. Figures 5-8 and 5-9 illustrate just two types of commonly used change-ups. They are generally regarded the easiest to learn and are most effective when perfected.

able to throw the change-up over the plate and near your intended spot. A change-up should always be thrown down around the knees—preferably away from the hitter.

Try to get the velocity of your change-up close to 15 miles per hour slower than your fastball. You can throw good change-ups that are 10 miles per hour slower, but 15 mph is an excellent goal. Over time, you should monitor the spin of your change-up and attempt to make it as close to the spin on your fastball as possible.

Figure 5-10. The change-up is held deep in the hand with the fingers around the ball to lessen the velocity.

Figure 5-11. Tom Seaver's fingers open after he releases the change-up. This action slows his arm and allows him the proper finish.

The Slider

The slider is a pitch that can be effective, but dangerous. As a result, you and your coach should be very careful when throwing this pitch. If you throw this pitch incorrectly, you can do great harm to your arm. You must be constantly aware of your release on this pitch and how the ball comes out of your hand. It is best not to attempt to throw a slider until after you reached high school age.

The main reason this pitch can be risky is the tendency to get your hand around the ball. Both the curveball and the slider should be thrown with your fingers on top of the ball, with no turning of your elbow. When the slider is thrown properly, your hand will still leave the ball to the outside of the ball. In other words, for a right-handed pitcher, the hand will leave the ball on the right side of the ball. It is extremely important that, like the curveball or any pitch, you do not spin your elbow or manipulate the ball. Do not try to spin the ball.

The slider is a pitch that should break across the plate approximately six inches. The ball will also have a small break downward when thrown properly. If your break is flat without any downward break, you are not staying on top of the ball.

You should grip the ball with your index and middle fingers above the ball. A seam should be on the outside of your middle finger. You should hold the ball slightly off-center to the outside of the ball, while your fingers are on top. (A right-hand pitcher should hold the right side of the ball as he stands behind the ball.) Your index finger should be immediately on top of the center of the ball, with your middle finger to the right of your index finger and touching your index finger.

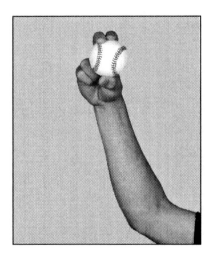

Figure 5-12. This photo shows a common grip for the slider. The fingers are placed on top of the ball to the outside of the ball with the middle finger along the seam. The thumb is under the ball. This grip causes your hand to rotate down outside of the ball at release, and enables you to spin the ball to break away and down from a right-hand hitter if you are a right-hand pitcher.

As you release the pitch, your fingers should release down to your landing foot, and you should feel the ball leave the inside of your hand. You must be careful not to turn the ball as it leaves your hand. Your middle finger will be your pressure point, and you should feel as if the top knuckle of your middle finger is throwing the ball downward. Because your finger is on top of the ball and slightly off-center, you do not need to spin the ball. It will naturally break down and across. If you feel your middle finger go straight down to the ground, you will have found the proper release for your slider.

If the ball breaks more than six inches, you are getting your hand too far to the side of the ball. This positioning is causing you to create a flatter, bigger break than you want with this pitch. With all pitches that you throw, remember that you want to get the ball to drop as it approaches the plate.

The Split-Finger Fastball

The split-finger fastball is the last pitch reviewed in this chapter. A good split will have the late drop that you are trying to achieve. The break is usually straight down, but it can sometimes break a little sideways at times. Because throwing this pitch can cause great harm to your delivery and deter from the effectiveness of your other pitches, you should use caution when deciding whether to use it.

The split-finger pitch is thrown with your index and middle finger split to both sides of the ball. It is held back in the knuckles of your fingers with your fingertips on the sides of the ball. Your thumb is below and in the middle of the ball.

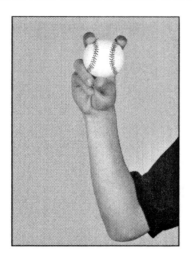

Figure 5-13. This photo shows a split-finger fastball grip, with the top two fingers spread to the outside of the two seams and the ball held back in the hand with the knuckles. The thumb is under the ball.

As you deliver the pitch, your fingers stay on the sides of the ball, and you simply throw a fastball, while staying over the top of the ball throughout your release. The higher your release point, the straighter down the ball will go. It should have a late break and drop almost straight down.

The drop of the split is later and sharper when you land a little stiffer and shorten your stride. You will have the feeling of being completely over your landing leg at release and throwing straight down.

The pitfall is that even Major League pitchers often shorten their stride and land stiffer as time goes on. These two bad habits create a tendency to throw other pitches

Figure 5-14. Donn Pall of the White Sox had a very good split-finger fastball. His index and middle fingers are spread on top of the ball with his thumb below the ball. Notice how far over his front leg his chest is. This factor helps the split drop.

with a stiff front leg and a stride that is too short. Other pitches will then lose their movement, and more pitches stay up in the strike zone.

Many split-finger pitchers develop sore elbows. It's not the split itself that causes these arm problems; it's only after throwing the other pitches with the aforementioned delivery flaw, that soreness can occur. This is why young pitchers should not throw this pitch. The other pitches reviewed in this chapter should give you plenty of options to get batters out.

While working on any pitch, it is important to remember that you do not want to turn your fingers sideways or manipulate the ball. The extension should be mainly your fingers extending to the target from on top of the ball.

Your fingers will naturally turn sideways at completion simply because your arm is attached to your body and must rotate around your landing leg. However, turning the ball too much or manipulating the ball as it leaves your hand can cause arm problems.

Pitches with Life

As you practice the pitches you have learned, you will notice that in the beginning, you will see some minor movement to the ball. As your delivery improves and you start to let go of the pitch rather than feel for it, you will notice that the break on your pitches will increase.

This increaase is attributed to the confidence you have at this point when throwing each pitch. You have a good idea how to throw the pitch and are confident enough to let it go. You will extend over your front leg better, the spin of the ball will be tighter, and thus you will begin to establish *life*.

Life is either natural or can be achieved from the processes that have been suggested. When you initially undertake an effort to be pitcher, your pitches will have movement by the grip you use and your natural throwing motion. As your confidence increases, your arm speed will naturally increase. As your arm speed increases, your extension through the finish will be more assertive. At that point, you will begin to notice a later movement to your pitches.

Arm speed and extension over a bent front leg are the ingredients needed for life. Do not try to turn the ball or manipulate it in any way to create life to your pitches. It is possible to create life if you learn the techniques illustrated in this book. All of these parts of your delivery are intended to create life, as you grow older. Maturity of your body is the most important creator of life. You must have the physical power and the proper mechanics to achieve life on the ball. You can only practice the proper techniques to get movement. When you get each pitch to move in the proper direction, you will have done all that you can do.

Figure 5-15. Mark Buehrle gets good extension over his front leg. The turning of his throwing arm is not intentional. Do not try to copy this. The hand normally goes this way on a fastbal,l and Buehrle is not manipulating the ball despite what it looks like.

As described previously, the curveball can have life in a downward direction. Because the ball is curled in your hand at release and your fingers are on top of the ball, the finish can create tight spin downward and create life to the curveball as well. As you gain confidence in throwing this pitch, you will find that you can throw it with maximum arm speed. If your mechanics, direction, and release are all correct, the ball will have a sharp break and be near the knees on the plate. I reached a point in my career where I felt I could throw my curveball with my eyes closed for strikes. This point illustrates how a correct delivery can maximize the effect and control of your pitches.

It is difficult to create life to the change-up because of the decrease in velocity. However, a change-up can have life if the sink or tail to the pitch is late, and the ball doesn't break until it nears the plate. This ball action will occur only after you have perfected your grip and can truly let the change-up go and not slow your arm and aim the ball. This is why you must work diligently on a grip for an effective change-up so that you can let it go without fear that it will be too fast. Your arm speed and finish will then allow the ball to move late, thus having life. Remember that *arm speed and finish create life*.

You will find that as the years go on and you throw all these pitches with confidence and the proper mechanics, you too will achieve life in your pitches. Don't be in a hurry to see life. Your pitches must have *all* of the ingredients on a consistent basis. Trust that over time, as you work on your delivery, it will come. *Use the same proper mechanics of throwing no matter what pitch you throw and extend over a bent front leg. Be consistent in your delivery and do not change it from pitch to pitch.*

Deception

One asset of a pitcher that has not been mentioned is deception. The methods described to this point in the book offer the most effective way to throw your pitches with power, movement, and control. The only negative that can result from the factors explained in this book is that they don't create deception.

With regard to pitching, deception is defined as the ability to deter the hitter from seeing the ball easily out of your hand and to prevent batters from timing your pitches. If you perfect your delivery, it is possible that you will look too *pretty* in the motion, and the hitter will be able to see the ball easily out of your hand.

The best way to create deception is to hide the ball from the hitter. If you have perfected your delivery, you can try a mild turn. As you lift your leg to go to the plate, turn your front leg slightly back toward second base. You must remember to keep your foot under your knee and not rotate too far back. Otherwise, you will lose your balance and come toward the plate sideways or spinning. Be careful not to spin out of your delivery or you will lose your downward plane.

A very slight rotation back is enough to take the ball behind your body, thus hiding the ball from the batter. As you make your circle behind you, the hitter will not see the ball until it gets over your throwing shoulder. As you attempt this, be sure to monitor yourself and not get too far back or cause yourself to sit on your back leg to maintain your balance. Making the baseball change planes, as well as working on a downward angle, are the two most effective ways to keep a hitter under control. The changing of speeds and locating the ball in the strike zone are other ways you can keep the hitter off balance.

Figure 5-16. Pedro Martinez has natural deception because of this slight turn over the rubber. This turn hides the ball from the hitter. His leg and hand mechanics are perfect despite the turn.

Because most young pitchers do not have the velocity to overpower hitters, they must develop other pitching skills. Even Major League power-strikeout pitchers will strike out only about 10 hitters a game when they are at the top of their game. Therefore, even these pitchers who are the best in the world must get 17 other outs by making the hitters get themselves out. *Keep in mind that while you can practice different ways of deception, you should never lose your balance or your direction to the plate.*

6

The Thinking Game

As you go about working on all of the mechanical moves in your delivery, it is important to remember that you must also focus on getting batters out. Literally following the directions in this book can make you too mechanical when you face a hitter.

While it is important that you diligently practice these factors on the sidelines, when you take the mound, you should focus on making pitches and getting hitters out. If you are in a game and thinking about where your feet and hands are, you will not be effective. You must draw the line between practice and performance, and be careful not to mix the two.

When you have the ball on the mound, the game doesn't begin until you are ready. Some acts, such as hitting a baseball, are reactionary—that is, you must react to a pitched ball and attempt to hit it. When you are pitching, you control when the game begins.

It is important that you collect your thoughts and focus on your plan before you toe the rubber. You should have a plan on how to attack the hitter, and focus on the catcher's glove. You should not be thinking about your mechanics or where you are going after the game. The more you can block out the rest of the world, the more capable you will be of winning. Keep it simple.

Strike one is the most important pitch you will throw. It is important to get the count in your favor and put the hitter on the defensive. He will then be forced to adjust to your pitches, rather than your limiting yourself as to what you can do. If you are 0-1 on the hitter, you have many options on what pitch you can throw and how much of the plate you have to throw the ball over. If you are 0-1, you can try new pitches without the fear of throwing a ball. Statistics indicate that as the count goes into the pitcher's favor (0-1, 0-2 or 1-2), batting averages go down. Then, you can make the hitters hit *your* pitch.

Conversely, if you are behind in the count (1-0, 2-0, 2-1 3-0 3-1), the hitter can narrow the zone in which he looks for the ball and look for a specific pitch. This situation occurs because most pitchers can't throw all of their pitches for strikes and usually have to come into the hitting zone with a fastball.

You can no longer go for the edges of the plate. As a result, you have to pitch over the heart of the plate. In turn, the hitter is much more likely to center the ball on the bat. Getting ahead in the count over the course of a game is the number one requisite of successful pitching. If you are consistently behind in the count, the hitters will eventually get to you as the game wears on.

The ability to throw strikes is the most important asset you can have in pitching. If the batter does not have to swing except when you lay the ball in, he will have the advantage. When you are batting, you know that you like the ball out over the plate, about thigh high. If you fall behind in the count, you will have to throw the ball to this area much more often. This is why getting ahead is of the utmost importance.

Concentrate on throwing the first pitch for a strike. The hitter is less prepared to hit and more unlikely to hit the first pitch as well as he will later in the count when he has seen all of your pitches. Do not fear contact on the first pitch.

The mechanics that have been discussed in this book will give you the ability not only to throw strikes, but also to locate your pitches to an area of the plate that is more difficult to hit. Hitters don't like when the ball is on the edge of the plate. They don't like it when the velocity is constantly changing or the plane of the pitch is changing. Getting ahead in the count and having the ability to throw different pitches for strikes arre the keys to success. Then, you can pitch to both sides of the plate or change the hitter's eye level by pitching high or low, in or out of the strike zone.

You must know what pitches you have that you have a good chance of throwing for strikes. A good pitch out of the strike zone does you no good unless you are ahead in the count, and the hitter is likely to chase a pitch that would be a ball. As a general rule, the fastball will be the pitch you can best throw for strikes. If the hitter you are facing is not one of the best in your opponent's lineup, you should be able to throw a first pitch fastball for a strike, and he shouldn't be able to center it on the bat.

Remember that hitters always have some uncertainty as to what pitch you will throw and where it will be. He is also seeing his first pitch, and it will be difficult to gauge the speed and movement of the pitch. It is best to be very aggressive with strikes early in the game and early in the count and let the hitters know that you aren't afraid to throw the ball over the plate.

If you show the ability to throw strikes, hitters will be more likely to come to the plate swinging. If you can then locate the ball to an area such as low and away or in on his hands, the hitter will be unable to react in time to hit the ball well.

Unless you have an overpowering fastball, it is best to hope for contact early in the count. You must keep in mind that the hitter is often anxious and, as such, will want to swing at the first pitch he thinks looks like a strike. He doesn't want to fall behind in the count. The perfect inning is three pitches for three outs, not three strikeouts. The strikeouts will take many more pitches and use up your energy for the rest of the game.

Of course, you want to stay away from the center of the plate and have the ability to pitch to the edges. You will be surprised how many outs you can get by locating a first-pitch fastball to a side of the plate and down in the strike zone. If you can get to a 0-1 count, your options are many. You can come back with another fastball to a different location or go back to the same place if you recognize a weakness. You can also throw any other pitch that you may feel is less likely to get hit without the fear of throwing a ball.

If you can get to a 1-2 or 0-2 count, then you can throw your most effective pitch, regardless if you think you can throw it for a strike. If you are behind, your options are limited. Hitters are much more likely to chase bad pitches when they are behind in the count. They will tend to be off-balance and just try to make contact rather than staying back and hitting the ball hard. Seven fielders are in the field with gloves, and they will catch most weakly hit balls.

As previously discussed, it is difficult, if not impossible, for an off-balanced hitter to drive the ball. Hitters who are ahead in the count are not often off-balance. To be successful you *must* be able to throw strikes when you need to.

When you hear talk about a plan or mental focus, it generally refers to your ability to concentrate on the task at hand. What pitch will you throw? Where would you like to throw that pitch? What are you hoping the hitter will do with that pitch? It is unrealistic to think that a hitter will swing and miss all pitches or stand there with the bat on his shoulder and watch all of your pitches go by. Every pitch you throw should have a purpose.

Are you hoping that the hitter will hit a groundball or a pop-up? Do you think he will take pitches until he gets a strike? What is the game situation? Will a simple ground ball score the go ahead run? What is the hitter trying to do? While these questions will be even more important as you get to high school, college, or pro baseball, it is essential that you keep these questions in mind as you pitch your game so you will improve over time.

Learn to *recognize* hitters. The first sign of how to attack a hitter is where he stands in the batter's box. If he stands away from the plate, he is telling you that he likes pitches that are away so he can extend his arms as he swings. You may be able to pitch him at the very outside corners of the plate, but he wants the ball on the outer half of the plate. Hitters who stand far away do not like the fastball inside near their hands. If they did, they'd stand nearer to the plate.

Conversely, the hitter who is near or on top of the plate likes the ball inside. He believes that he has quick enough hands to catch up to the inside fastball. While it is best to attack him on the outside half of the plate, you must also show him that you will come inside and back him off of the plate occasionally. It is possible that you will hit some hitters with the pitch, but you must show them you can pitch inside. If you do not pitch them inside, they will have control of the plate with no fear and be able to reach any pitch you throw.

The ability to pitch inside is one of the most important assets that a pitcher can have in his repertoire. If you are to be a successful pitcher, hitters must know that you can and will throw the ball inside on and off the plate. If the hitter has no fear of getting hit with the ball, he will dig in and attack any pitch you throw. You must acquire the ability to throw on the inside part of the plate for strikes, pitch inside off the plate, and have enough control to not hit the batter with the pitch.

After you have thrown a pitch and the hitter has taken the pitch or has swung and missed, take a look at how he is standing. Has he opened up his front foot and tried to pull the ball? Did he dive out over the plate? Was he late to react to a fastball?

If a hitter has opened his front foot to pull the ball, he wants the ball on the inner part of the plate. It is best to stay on the outside part of the plate, as he will then pull off the pitch and not be able to drive the ball. It is just as important with this type of hitter to throw a fastball or two in off the plate to back him away from the plate to set up the outside pitch. Because he needs to be concerned that you may come way inside and maybe hit him, he will be on his heels and not reach the outside pitch you come back with. Be able to see if he makes corrections or stays the same with each at bat.

If he strides and gets his front foot closer to the plate as he strides, he is looking for a pitch to get his hands out and drive the ball up the middle or to the opposite field. Therefore, he will have a difficult time handling the pitch that is in on his hands.

If you can get ahead in the count, you can waste a pitch outside that he can't reach and then come back inside. This sequence will confuse him, and he won't know where you are going next. If you fall behind in the count, you will probably be unable to throw to a spot and will give him something he can hit.

If he has a slow bat or is late on your fastball, you do not want to throw something slower to give him the chance to catch up to the ball. It is not the proper time to try to trick him. Rather, you should go right after him with hard stuff up and down and not worry about changing speeds. Be aggressive and challenge him until he shows you he can catch up to your fastball.

The hitter and your own abilities should dictate to you what is the best plan of attack. You will find that if you have a better-than-average velocity, most teams at your level would have four to six hitters who can't handle your fastball if you change locations. If this is true, you will have more success staying with your hard stuff and having a plan of up and down rather than in and out.

It is not necessary to be too fine with the pitch. Your *stuff* alone should be enough to get your opponents out as long as you don't throw the ball down the middle of the plate. You will find that recognizing hitters will make pitching much easier if you have the ability to locate the ball.

Remember that you *must* throw the ball *through* the glove, not *to* the glove. If you aim the ball to the target, you will lose velocity and movement. Let your natural ability take over and always stay within yourself.

Don't try to throw harder than you can. Your mechanics and performance will suffer. When a pitch is located on the outside corner at the knees or on the hands inside, it is difficult to hit the ball hard unless the hitter knows where the pitch will be. You can make a hitter look foolish with a well-thrown change-up if you have set this pitch up by throwing fastballs.

If you don't focus on making the hitter swing and miss all the time, you can let the hitter get himself out. Every pitch does not need to be perfect, but you must use the last pitch thrown as an indicator for the next one.

If you find a zone a certain hitter cannot handle, stay in that zone until he shows you he can adjust and hit that pitch. For example, if you throw an outside fastball down in the strike zone and he doesn't take a very good swing at it, stay there with the next pitch. Stay as close to that area of the plate as you can until he shows you the ability to adjust to that pitch.

It is not necessary to throw something different and *trick* the batter. The better the hitter is, the more you need to have different pitches that change planes or locate to a place in the zone that he can't get the fat part of the bat on the ball. Pitching is indeed an art, and success depends on your ability to master the art.

You will never find an absolute way to get hitters out, but if you can see what the hitter is trying to do you can begin a plan of attack. It is important to think about what the last pitch did, rather than what it was meant to do.

For example, if you were trying to throw a fastball inside to the hitter, but the ball was on the outside corner, you should decide where to throw the next pitch based on how the hitter reacted. Did he react well to where you threw the pitch? Can you go back to the same place, or did he seem to be right on the pitch? Should you go inside to get him off the plate?

The aforementioned factors are all considerations that you and your catcher should recognize and adjust to accordingly. It is not always necessary to go to a different place in the strike zone if the hitter didn't look as if he were able to handle the last pitch. More often than not, however, you can come inside after an outside fastball and keep him guessing on what you will do next.

If you are able to throw other pitches, such as a change-up or curveball, these pitches are most effective after an inside fastball. This practice is called setting up your pitches.

Not every pitch you throw should be a strike to get a hitter out. If you throw a good inside fastball for a strike, you have shown him your velocity, and the batter will be very ready for the next pitch. He will generally be anxious because the ball was near him, and you probably injected some fear in him. A change-up or curveball will tend to fool him more if it follows this pitch. Fooling a hitter is surprising him and upsetting his timing and getting him off-balance. As a general rule, it is not a good practice to try to fool too many hitters. If you do try to fool the hitter, the best time to attempt this is after an inside fastball.

The hitter's reaction to any pitch should give you good insight on how you can get him out. You should be able to tell if you can overpower him with fastballs. If he is on your fastball or fouls the ball straight back, he probably has your pitch timed, and it is a good idea to throw a pitch at a different velocity.

If he pulls the ball foul, he is early and will have difficulty adjusting to a change-up. If he doesn't cover the outside part of the plate, you can stay outside on him until he shows you he will adjust and stay over the plate longer.

You must be the person who sees how the hitter reacts to the pitch. It is up to you to see if one zone or pitch exists that this particular hitter cannot handle or if you need to mix in different pitches or throw the ball to different areas of the plate.

Unless you see a specific weakness in the hitter, it is always a good idea to throw the next pitch to the opposite part of the plate than the last one. The more unsure he is of where you will throw the ball, the less he can guess a pitch or a location.

Most effective pitchers generally throw the ball around the knees. The farther the ball is from the hitter's eyes, the more difficult it is to center the ball on the bat. Most hitters have trouble with the ball on the outside quarter of the plate and knee high. While this is not always true, it gives you a starting point in your plan to get hitters out. This place is where you should attack first if you do not know the batter.

You should always pitch down and away until the hitter shows you he can hit that pitch. If you have the ability to throw the ball in that location, you will always enjoy some success. However, some hitters will be able to adjust to your pitch. If they are able to adjust to the pitch thrown low and away, it is an indication that you should try different locations or different pitches.

If you have good control and like to pitch down in the strike zone, it is important occasionally to throw one up out of the strike zone, eye high. This practice is called changing sightlines and will make your low pitches more effective.

The better the hitter, the more different looks you must be able to show him to get him out. Don't give the hitter too much credit, however. Hitting a pitched baseball is still the one of the hardest thing to do in sports.

While addressing hitters' tendencies and ways to attack hitters, it is important to remember that you will be much more successful if you focus on your own strengths as a pitcher rather than just the hitter's weaknesses. It is very helpful to watch hitters and identify means to get them out. However, it is more important to stay within yourself and try only those things that have a relatively good chance of being successful.

Know your strengths and weaknesses. What pitches do you throw well? Do not throw pitches you think the hitter is weak on if you yourself are not capable of throwing those pitches. For example, if you know the hitter is susceptible versus change-ups, you shouldn't throw one if you slow down your arm or can't throw one for strikes.

You must stay with the things with which you can succeed. If the choice is between a pitch you throw well or one that the batter has trouble with, you should throw *your* pitch. Your strengths will always be more effective than simply trying to attack a hitter's weakness.

It is the battle between pitcher and hitter that is the intriguing part of baseball and keeps people's attention. Preventing the hitter from hitting the ball squarely on the bat is the pitcher's main goal.

As a young pitcher, it is enjoyable and very thought provoking to watch Major League pitchers and catchers working the ball around the zone and changing speeds and choosing pitches to make the batter uncomfortable. You can gain great insight if you watch a game from behind the pitcher and guess along concerning the pitcher's selection of pitches and locations.

Strike one is the most important pitch you can throw. Learn to pitch inside for strikes and balls. Always pitch to your strengths ahead of the hitter's weaknesses.

7

A Balancing Act

Some coaches believe a parallel exists in the mechanics of pitching and those involved in the golf swing. Those of you who have played golf can understand that as you stand over the ball you have your feet directly under your shoulders. If you haven't played golf, watch a professional golfer on television. The golfer attempts to get as balanced and relaxed as possible while addressing the ball. The hands are in front of the waist as the club is behind the ball. The feet are shoulder-width apart and the shoulders square.

You should attempt to get into the same position as you reach the balance point of your pitching delivery over the rubber. The more balance you have in golf, the straighter the golf ball will go. This situation is the same in pitching. As you swing the club behind your body, your weight shifts to your back leg. It is important that while you swing the golf club, you do not lose the balance you had while addressing the ball. The same factor holds true when pitching.

The law of physics states that for every action you make, an opposite and equal reaction occurs. Therefore, if you lose your balance point or swing too far back in the arm swing either with a golf club or a baseball, you must overcompensate as you swing forward.

Since you feel you get more power if you swing back farther, it is a natural tendency to take the ball too far back when throwing. If you make this common mistake, it will cause you to rotate too far and make you spin around your target. You can lose balance and fail to drive toward your target. As you shift your weight to your front foot in the golf swing and your hands come through to hit the ball, you drive your power through your front leg.

If you are balanced over your front leg on the golf swing, you will be accurate to the target. You then extend your hands upward and finish in a balanced position, and finish high.

Because the golf swing is an underhand move, you extend up and finish high. The pitching motion, on the other hand, is overhand. Therefore, your finish is downward to the ground and extends over your front leg to the ground. These moves are similar in that the keys to success in both are balance and extension to the front side. If you lose the balance at any point over your back leg and your swing gets too long, you will have to make the opposite reaction on the front side, and it will cause you to lose direction to the target.

Pitching, as in golf, is a combination of power and control, and you cannot sacrifice either. The art of combining these two skills is one of the keys to success in either endeavor. This factor is why the mechanics of pitching have been stressed in this book to such a great degree. As in golf, the power comes from the speed in which you drive your hands and arms in the motion, not how far you take your hand back.

The shorter the arm swing and the closer your hand to your body, the more power you generate. One illustration that can help you understand is if you were to try to punch a punching bag as hard as you could, you would not take a long full swing but rather get extension as you draw your arm back.

As you come forward with your punching hand, you would extend your arm out front and drive through the target. This approach would enable you to deliver the most power. If you would take your hand too far back, your arm has a long swing and does not achieve maximum velocity. If you keep your hand too close to your body, you can only jab and not get full extension in the back or out front. This scenario is the same pitching action that is commonly referred to as *short-arming*, which is getting your hand too close to your shoulder and not properly extending through the target.

Shooting a basketball or throwing a bowling ball or hitting a tennis ball are all actions best achieved by being balanced through your arm swing and having your feet underneath and at shoulder-width apart.

I am constantly amazed that the best pro golfers are always calling their teachers to watch their swing through the ball to monitor any defects in their swing. Over the past several years, it seems baseball has gotten away from this analytical approach to pitching. Off-balance pitchers are often seen flying off the mound. In turn, many arm problems resulting from bad deliveries. Pitchers in general are less effective, their control is lacking, and arm problems are common. This situation has attributed to an accompanying rise in Major League batting averages and runs scored. In my opinion, pitchers have lost their ability to concentrate on proper techniques.

Tiger Woods may be the best golfer of all time, yet he is constantly trying different things with his swing and his hands through the swing. He has his swing coach with him wherever he is to analyze his swing. If arguably the best golfer in the world believes he needs his swing monitored so often, why is it that most pitchers do not want to analyze their motion? Such an analysis can enable them to become more consistent.

Without question, professional athletes strive to be consistent and attempt to employ their natural talents to the best of their ability in the competitive sports arena. Videotape has become an important tool. If you can take the things you've learned in this book and then see yourself on film, you will be better prepared to dissect your own delivery and make many of the necessary corrections as you go. By the same token, having a coach who also understands the proper delivery mechanics and techniques will help you be more consistent and will further your development as a pitcher.

Pitching involves the same athletic attributes you use in all other sports. Keep your balance and direct your power to the target.

Epilogue

Remember that pitching is a continual journey to success, and you will always have constant corrections to make. You may never achieve the perfect delivery, but if you can be controlled throughout the process, you will have success. Time and experience will teach you the proper way for you to pitch, and it will not seem as complicated or exact as time goes on. Do not become frustrated during the process.

Any endeavor takes time and hard work. Consistency and success will come and be easier to achieve over time. Pitching a baseball is not an exact science, but the closer you get to perfecting this delivery the better your chances of becoming a successful pitcher.

Some of the factors that have been discussed in this book may be too advanced for you. It is important to discuss the points covered in this book with your parents or your coach and recognize when it is right for you to try them. While I have attempted to keep the presentation of the information relatively simple, some of the mechanics can get quite complicated at times. Hopefully, you will repeat the points and exercises until you understand them.

The mechanics reviewed in this book can be initiated as early as age 10. As you get older and grow, you can refer to and practice some of the more advanced teachings. Get your coach to read this book so that he will understand what you are trying to accomplish. He can watch you and help you advance as you progress.

The basics of this book are directed at someone who throws from a high, three-quarter delivery or overhand. If that is where your release is from, all of the points covered in this book can help you. If your release is different, then you must decide which parts of the book are appropriate for you. No matter what your release point is, balance and one power move to the plate are always important to achieve.

Hopefully, this book will be a great teaching tool for aspiring pitchers. Perhaps, I will be fortunate enough to get feedback from the readers as time goes on. When you make it to the Major Leagues, make sure you let me know if this book helped you in the process. Baseball is a great game and a great way to make a living. Good luck and I wish you all the greatest success.

Learn the delivery described in this book as completely as possible. Refer back to all of the chapters as you grow and incorporate new ideas as you mature. Be watchful of other pitchers you see, and continue to analyze your own pitching technique.

About the Author

Larry Monroe is the Chicago White Sox vice president of free agent and Major League scouting, a position he has held since October 1994. Prior to assuming his present position, He served as the White Sox's vice president of scouting and minor league operations from 1990 to 1994.

A former right-handed pitcher for the Chicago White Sox, Monroe has 29 years of experience with the White Sox organization as a player, scout, minor league instructor, and coach. He served as both a special assistant to the general manager and major league scout before taking over vice president duties.

A graduate of Forest View High School in Arlington Heights, Illinois, Monroe received all-conference baseball honors three times and all-area baseball honors twice. He was the White Sox number one selection in the June 1974 free agent draft and made his Major League debut with the White Sox on August 23, 1976, in Detroit, where he pitched two scoreless, hitless innings.

Monroe is married to Jaine and has three children: Taylor, Allison, and Grant, and two stepchildren: Alexandra and Rachael.